D1524878

Dancing on the Edges of Knives

DANCING ON THE
EDGES OF KNIVES

Poems by

Ed Ochester

A Breakthrough Book
University of Missouri Press
Columbia
1973

Acknowledgments

Beloit Poetry Journal: "The Fat Man in the Easy Chair"

Centennial Review: "King Kong"

Chicago Review: "Facts about Death"; "My Penis"; "My Teeth"

Colorado Quarterly: "Dialog"; "A Short Life"

Crazy Horse: "The Gift"; "James Wright Walks into a Sumac Patch near Aliquippa, Pennsylvania"

Descant: "Anna Bachtle" (under the title "The Air Plant")

Hanging Loose: "August of '62"; "For You"; "Machismo"; "Note for Door"

Happiness Holding Tank: "A Very Dedicated Poet"

Hearse: "Karin"; "Variations on a Piece by Brautigan"

The Midwest Quarterly: "Children's Books"

New: "To the Werewolf Committee"

The New Republic: "The Knute Rockne Story." Reprinted by permission of *The New Republic*, © 1973 Harrison-Blaine of New Jersey, Inc.

Nimrod (1967) and *Best of* Nimrod (1970): "Evolution"

Open Places: "Ordinary Evening"; "Robert Bly Watched by Elves"

Perspective: "Daytona Beach Concert"; "Shop Sign"

Poetry Northwest: "Among His Effects We Found a Photograph"; "When the Dow Jones Industrial Index Hit Its All-Time High in 1966"

Prairie Schooner: "The Inheritance"; "Stanzas on Owls" (under the title "Eight Stanzas on Owls"); "A Vision of Collegiate Nuns." Copyright © 1967, 1971, by the University of Nebraska Press

Quixote: "At Kingston"; "Daytona Beach Concert"; "Dialog"; "The Gift"; "A Line of Patchen's"; "Robert Bly Watched by Elves"; "A Short Life"; "A Vision of Collegiate Nuns"; "Zeno's Arrow"

Trace: "A Line of Patchen's." Copyright © 1970, by *Trace* No. 71

TransPacific: "Collective Guilt"

West Coast Review: "Ad Hoc Poem for the Winter Solstice and for Bob Levine"

Western Humanities Review: "In the Library"

Wormwood Review: "Morte d'Arthur"; "Nine Ways to Have a Good Time in Pittsburgh" (under the title "9 Ways of Having a Good Time in Pittsburgh"); "Zeno's Arrow"

ISBN 0–8262–0153–9
Library of Congress Catalog Number 73–85458
Printed and bound in the United States of America
Copyright © 1973 by Ed Ochester

This Book is for Britt,
Morris Edelson,
and The Grateful Dead

The Devins Award for Poetry

Dancing on the Edges of Knives won, in manuscript, The Devins Award for Poetry for 1973, the major prize of the Kansas City Poetry Contests.

Ed Ochester's manuscript was chosen from several hundred collections submitted anonymously by poets across the nation. Judges for the 1973 competition were Michael Harper and Mark Strand.

The annual Award is made possible by the generosity of Dr. and Mrs. Edward A. Devins. Dr. Devins is former President of the Kansas City Jewish Community Center and is a patron of the Center's American Poets Series.

Contents

I

On a Friend Whose Work Has Come to Nothing

At school you dove off the bridge at night
in a swan, down to the half-dozen girls
treading water to keep up with you.
Then, cock of the walk, you'd strut off
with some chick while the rest of us
were left to drink lukewarm beer and cluck.

Those were the Dylan Thomas days when
wearing baggy tweeds you picked up west of Wales
you told *Under Milk Wood* so that all the dead below
were wet with tears. Then
you'd cut out with a casual girl
and leave us to dismantle the scene.

There were also the Norman Mailer days,
the quiet admonitions to suck the smoke in deep,
the blue morning jogs around the lake.
You were the last descendant of the
        Grand Duke Maximilian,
and every one of us was the true illegitimate
son of Hemingway, who
by the way,
was your very close friend.

You made yourself the prince of days
because you cracked imagination's cipher;
you taught us to ignore the telegrams
from the past that never came,
found at the heart of our onion
the nothing you'd been sure was there.
So. Our banquets and our pioneer characters
were spun from the brightness in the air.

Christ, while the rest of us thought each thud
of our typewriters was tough enough
        to puncture hearts,
you heard America snapping its gum
and laughed and fluted tunes
through their public forests
on the coast of pacific despair.

Thus, seeing a one-inch notice of your death
in a small-town Midwest paper,
it is difficult to say exactly what death
        has taken in,
except assuredly a politician among the apes,
a hummingbird above the snails.

But the rest of us—
Lord, vaguely amazed at your death,
corrupt as you but less successful,
still losing twenty dreams a year
        like irreplaceable feathers—
the rest of us at least two thousand miles
        behind you
are still crawling outward toward
        our mythical west coast.

When the Dow Jones Industrial Index
Hit Its All-Time High in 1966

Just then children began to disappear,
just then blood began to accumulate in the lowlands,
springs of blood resumed their flow
in Kansas and Mississippi,
blood pooled
in Chicago, Dallas, Los Angeles.
Just then supertankers of blood
began to arrive from Asia
to pump their cargo
into the harbors and streets of the cities.
And even in the small cities
and on the failing farms
men slept at night
like caged wolves,
smelling blood in their dreams,
tiny bubbles of blood
welling up in their nostrils.

After Advertising Ended

small children starved to death,
mothers did not know how to lactate
and wore brassieres over their eyes,
telephone wire was cut into belts and ties,
airplanes were worshiped
and cars lathered with acne lotion;
thousands of women migrated into the Atlantic,
    singing,
and bewildered young lovers
tentatively put their thumbs in their ears.

Collective Guilt

One day
the Indian population went wild
expanding like yeast in
an agar dish bulging
beyond their reservations
and this went on
until there were five Indians
for every white man
and they proceeded
to kick the shit out of the white wickiups
massacring the pitiful wives wailing in huddles
torturing old men suspected
of sympathizing with their sons
napalming Cheyenne Wyoming
and Sioux City Iowa
in order to save them.
And one old white philosopher
about to be flayed alive
asked "Why do you do this Kimasabee?
I never even seen an Indian before
no less been cruel to one,"
and a malignant buck with a dozen
bald scalps at his buckle
answered
"Well tough tittie man nothing personal
but this ain't the land of the fair
it's the home of the braves
and moreover
in a generation or two
my kids will be absolved
of all guilt."

Dialogue

I'm sorry that I have misjudged you.
Your slaughter of the innocents
led me astray. An old professor
put the worst possible interpretation on it.

Forgive me for the time
I said you were mistaken
when you bombed the infants' hospital.
I see now that you have averted war.

When you machine-gunned the five thousand cripples
I questioned the wisdom of your action,
but now I find it was to protect my job.

I was a fool to suggest you misled us
in the campaign against mental defectives.
It has preserved our way of life.

Now that I understand you
I wonder about nothing,
except where the next threat
is to come from.

Nine Ways to Have a Good Time in Pittsburgh

attend an "over 21" dance at the Webster Hall Hotel

listen to Archibald MacLeish read at the International
    Poetry Forum

walk around the Stephen Foster Memorial

read the entertainment section of *The New York Times*

see the steel mills at night two nights in a row
                          two nights in a row

walk around Mellon Square

walk the other way around Mellon Square

take a taxi through the suburbs of Weirton, McKees
        Rocks, Millvale, Blawnox, Etna, Rankin,
        Homestead, Dravosburg, Beltzhoover, and
        Wilmerding

guess which the Monongahela River?
                       and which
    the Allegheny?

King Kong

To be seriously maladjusted
is to despise organization.
You were a fool
to break your chains so easily
and to pull that grandstander
against the Army Air Force.
Grunting and loving women
are enough handicaps.
With planning you could have become
the general in charge of skyjacking
or a vice-presidential possibility.
Democratic hopefuls would have
begged for endorsements,
and housewives lusted
for your gigantic body.

The trick
when one sees their society for the first time
is to restrain the primal scream of horror,
to dream of islands,
but to go along.

To the Werewolf Committee

Who is the sad werewolf wandering
around Central Park Lake?

Why does he drool behind trees
to frighten the honey-haired girls
as they walk
toward wealthy marriages?

Why does he threaten
Professor Kavounas
as he absorbedly studies
the ecology of ducks?

Gentlemen,
as a member of the mayor's Commission on
      Werewolves
I say, before we ring him over the snout
with our authorized crucifix,
just once let us talk to him.
Not much can be expected of werewolves,
since we know it's their nature to threaten and drool,
but let us, let us at least offer to get him
an honorable job in a traveling side-show
or in the stock room at F. A. O. Schwarz.
Thus, if only for the sake of experiment
or to say "We have done as much as we can,"
let us throw an arm around him
or even offer to buy him a beer
before, as we shall undoubtedly have to,
we drive him back to his pit in the zoo.

August of '62

I'm sitting in the precinct house
on Cross Bay Boulevard. The detective sergeant
flips through a *Playboy*, stops at the centerfold.
"Tellya how bad it is kid,
they piss out the winders whenya walk downa street.
Even the jews startin amove."
Here's lookin at you, kid.

I'd like to see those pictures in his drawer.

Two cops bring in a kid and throw him in the cage.
No shirt. Blood on his shoulder.
Smiling in shock. Or smiling. "Cocksuckers."
The cops move toward him. The wound
with its tiny puckered lips, the blood
the rose of great peace.

The Penn Central Station at Beacon, N. Y.

An immense room as quiet
as an elephant graveyard
without spines or tusks.
Dust in the slantlight from windows
twenty feet up the wall.
Yesterday's *Times* for sale.
The stationmaster in a green eyeshade
snoozing or dead.
Below the clock an American flag.
Twice a day empty trains
go by without stopping—
Eisenhower Eisenhower Eisenhower Eisenhower—
one-eyed trains twice a night—
FDR & FDR & FDR & FDR—
shuttle between
Albany Albany Albany Albany
Manhattan Manhattan Manhattan Manhattan

The Knute Rockne Story

Shouldn't the *K* be pronounced?
If not, his parents could have called him
Pnute, Gnute, Fnute, or Babbaganute.
His mother was toying with Rock Knutne,
but they decided on Knute Rockne
with a silent *K*.
If the Gipper's parents had done this,
they could have named him the Kipper,
the Zipper, the Ripper, or the Dipper.
None of this happened,
according to the movie.
I can never remember who the Gipper
was. Ronald Reagan? Iron Horseman?
I can barely remember Rock Knutne.
I loved football, and this is what it has done for me:
Thousands of letters lost in the mail,
our country's history an incomplete forward pass.

Children's Books

In the world more real,
the goosegirl is dropped to the ashes,
the crystal valley is bombed and its shards
rebombed by invisible planes,
the adorable kittens are drowned
along with their friend,
the crazy nice useless old lady.

In their dreams of life, children
arrive at the reasons
like the beanstalk seemingly fated
to meet the bloodthirsty giant.
Meanwhile, they keep their books
because the stories tell them
what to do if
the Japanese princess
with twelve golden bears
shyly knocks at their door.

Ad Hoc Poem for the Winter Solstice
and for Bob Levine

Today, Levine, I sat down to write you.
I wanted to tell you about the things I've seen
from my window—the neighbor's son
(scratching the ice from his walk)
whose highest ambition after twenty-six years
is to raise his degrees and get kids,
the tree in front of the window whose leaves
turn yellow in a second and green
again the next as I watch.
Do you know that I often remember
the empty Beefeaters' bottle that
was tossed through your window the night
that Fred sprayed your rotten peach punch
over the floating dregs of the party?
That's why I love you—
as a person sinking through my common ground.
I have forgotten nothing of inconsequence,
and consequential things,
like dew on the cold steel of the tractor,
I begin to condense and collect.
In the Midwest, I lift my finger,
and the world
falls into place like a kaleidoscope.
This is why I've been meaning to ask whether
the world is exactly what you meant it to be.
That is, the elms roll off to market,
the rains come down,
the hens crawl out intelligently to squat
for their lovers in the scrabbling grass
as our golden chickens, content with the Jefferson
        Airplane,
forget how to fly back home to roost.

Levine, like a rooster on his dung heap
I look blindly at the sun through the snowfall
and begin, with my usual wing-flap,
the orchestration of windmills and pigs.
You asked me whether I don't underestimate myself,
and I ask you
does the rooster know if he can fly?

II

A Vision of Collegiate Nuns

Nuns everywhere!
blowing in and out of libraries,
clopping up the hill through snowflakes
like black tongue-muffled bells—
sweet smiling sour scowling nuns
intimidating seminars,
dumbfounding wanton sparrows,
philosophical nuns marching straight to the roof-edge
        of rough doctrine,
literary nuns swirling in worldly figures,
historical nuns glaring disapproval of mass murder.
Having gotten from their nunnery, do they
hear words no ear has heard,
see sights no eye has seen?
Who can believe it or afford not to believe it?
O sisters of us all,
busy black grapes
the world is forever trying to spoil,
how can any voice in this whirlwind
sing you anything but ridicule and praise?

In the Library

the silent girl,
the ugly one,
waits out the spring above her books;
her thoughts poise between
pleasures in the strong sun
and the despair her fragile body brings.

She is the white crane
staring downward,
conscious of her reed neck
that the smallest stone can break.

The Fat Man in the Easy Chair

reads his verse aloud.
Mincing gestures and a florid face
have captured a college crowd. Two quite in-
tent young girls smile nervously; sniggering
softly, some better poets rim the room;
an obliged professor yawns secretly.
But most will leave the exhibition
enriched and gratified that over coffee
they can talk about their subject, poetry.

The huge fingers of evening enter
the smoky room, touch and merge the meager
faces, darken the thin sad skin.
                                        Pigeons,
somersaulting, catch the last cold rays
of the bloody sun, glint the empty bowl,
the thin, the distant blue. Through a window,
one magnifies, glides smoothly to the ledge,
softly, coos, struts, puffs his iridescence.
He ignores the stuffy room; the fat man
puffs his cheeks, ignores the easy pigeon.

Trope

In college Irony won a medal
for the 100–yard dash.
He still wears an athletic supporter
but now travels on package tours,
sneering "Show me"
as he runs past the monuments.
His favorite food is sour kidneys;
water is his only drink.
Every morning he spends hours
carefully parting his hair in the middle
and choosing fashionable clothes.
Though he refuses to disclose
his means of support,
he is a frequent and well-paid speaker
at second-rate universities, board meetings,
advertising agencies, and charity hospitals.
His secret shame is that he is a virgin
through fear.
His greatest pleasure is to secretly mock
old women, adolescents, prophets, and martyrs.
If threatened by the earnest and indignant,
he will cheerfully slit his own throat.

A Very Dedicated Poet

says to me,
"I would rather write a poem
than screw,
and in fact
I am right now
in the throes of composition
writing a piece about
getting laid."

James Wright Walks into a Sumac Patch near Aliquippa, Pennsylvania

Just off the highway to Aliquippa, Pennsylvania,
smog billows forth on the grass.
And the eyes of two puppies
moisten with kindness.
They stumble out of the sumac,
where they have been playing alone, all day.
They quiver expectantly; they can hardly contain
    their happiness
that we are coming.
They jump shyly as little girls. They love each other.
There is no loneliness like theirs.
I would like to hold the big fellow in my arms,
for he has walked over to me
and nuzzled my left
hand.
He is black and white.
The skin inside his thigh
is delicate as the skin behind a girl's
thorax.
Suddenly I realize
that if I stepped out of my body, I would melt
into puddles.

Robert Bly Watched by Elves

On snowy evenings I like to
drive downtown to place my
cheek against the steel
of our Midwestern mailbox.

Tonight I receive illumination
from the street lamps
as I lie in snow
surrounded by elves

lifting their arms, *Salud*!
Their mittens are filled with snow.
The snow is shaped into balls.
Now the elves run from a ghostly

snowplow plowing through
snow toward us. It is good
to lie in snow, seeing things
invisible to impure men.

A Short Life

As a young scholar, he taught
the sophomore lecture on Knowledge;
tenured, he inherited
the graduate survey of Wisdom,
where, when he spoke,
he frequently burst into tears.
One day his son burned down the library,
and he wondered
"Have I ever known anything, at all?"
At the end of his life,
the University of Central La Brea
made him Honorary Fossil
and put him behind glass in a case,
where now he amuses young mummies
whose brains and intestines are missing and
who are incapable of children besides.

Stanzas on Owls

Friends told him
owls are good for mice,
but he crucified owls
like thieves
and smiled with the ancient wisdom
of the farmer.

Aunt Adassa
had a stuffed owl named Wallace
whom she was pleased to call "lover"
but who rarely replied.

Comb the grass.
Pulps like raspberries
attest
some owls
cannot be stopped by fences.

They digest gristle
and bone;
owls have good bowels.

Ravens attack owls
in daylight,
but it is not therefore
to be assumed
that ravens
are nobler than owls.

The owl's beak
is as bent
as an old crone's toenail.
In the daylight
he rests his beak
upon his paunch
and sleeps.

The owl
at the Brookfield Zoo
is wise.
He regards his captors calmly,
grips his branch,
and continues to think his thoughts.

Owls make love
gravely
as though the world
depended upon
the eggs of owls.

Variations on a Piece by Brautigan

After Polonius snuffed out Ophelia's indiscretion,
there was silence for a week in Darien. Laertes was
true to himself and his ambition to be first-string
guard at Yale by doing pushups and studying his
hair in a mirror. Polonius in his brown study chortled
and perused Dean Acheson, George Kennan, and
Arthur Schlesinger and wrote policy briefs. Meanwhile, upstairs, altogether elsewhere, Ophelia decided
to become a human being. Week by week she
watched the smoky moon and learned to hate and
studied how a puppet might burn her strings. With her
last remaining Avon lipstick she wrote "Polonius
is a schmuck" on her brassiere and then destroyed it.
She sang to herself all the dirty songs she knew;
unfortunately, she only knew two so was forced to
make some up. She imagined "sinning" till she shriveled like a penis she had seen a line drawing of in a
health education manual. She read Rupert Brooke and
Edna St. Vincent Millay from the old books bequeathed
her by her sad mother, Rosamona, who had died in
her infancy of boredom. But all the while, like a
politic child, she kept her fire beneath a blanket, still
saying fairly, "I will obey, my lord," and "I think
nothing, sir."

So that very fall, trundled off to Radcliffe, she
had a store of wicked experiments to try. She started
small, smoked a little "Acapulco Gold!" and was
deflowered unceremoniously by an offspring of the
Teledyne Research Professor at Tufts the very week
she won the Josiah Royce Freshman Essay Medal by
showing that Roy Earle, the ex-con Bogart plays in
High Sierra, is the model for the mad businessman
Roy Earle in Brautigan's *Confederate General*, which
went to show that Denmark was a prison. But search-
ing through inversions she grew warmer, began to
smoke, suck, sniff, or sleep with any novelty, though

she was happiest for a fortnight with a group of
wandering players from New York who called her
"Fortune's Wheel" and "the Witch Lady of Brattle"
and used her in their act as the bawdy hand of time.
And then hundreds came to warm themselves before
her burning, since the incineration of a life is more
narcotic than the fume of poppies. And yet she still
dreamed about a shriveled scrap of paper lost among
her ancient toys that said "Doubt thou the stars
are fire, but never doubt I love," so after the telegram
came to tell her that scrutable Polonius had died of
a ruptured appendix, the few who knew her best
felt a sense of *déjà vu* the afternoon after the morning she had distributed what she said was rosemary,
sage, parsley, and thyme when she threw herself
from the Pepperpot Bridge in her heavy homespun,
so that Laertes blundered up from Yale and practice
to lament:

> "Alas, then she is drown'd!
> Too much of water has thou, poor Ophelia."

Karin

Still to be neat, still to be dressed
as you were going to your daily test.

Still

> quoting Kahlil Gibran
> grooving on Freudian slips
> taking *The Times*
> lighting skinny candles
> reading introductions
> arguing pot pro and con
> discussing Marshall McLuhan
> trying to dig Stockhausen
> refusing to keep a canary
> wearing a strapless bra
> going to John Ciardi lectures
> summering in Wellfleet
> drinking Heineken
> writing haiku
> using Dial
> contributing to the United Negro College Fund
> hating conformity
> eating Dannon Yogurt
> praising Pope John
> explaining the errors of Marx

after all these years still
coming home still
lonely still
superior still
waiting still
about to

For You

How sad to be a casual girl,
how sad to be bounced
in the rear of station wagons
along the shores of shrunken lakes.
How sad to listen to the men play
blackjack in the cabin and believe
Kafka's *Castle* is a hamburger joint
and Truffaut a kind of mushroom.
How sad never to understand anything at all.
How sad to walk along the lake at night
and not understand why the stars have all
been eaten by the god whose name you
forget at the moment but whom
Tibetans try to frighten with bells, cymbals,
and hideous dances on the edges of knives.
How sad to return to the cabin
and find the dead goose hung to bleed,
clamps in its nostrils, spinning
clockwise, counterclockwise—
that beautiful body hung like meat,
dribbling blood truly toward
the center of gravity.

Love Story

I climbed the stairs
to your apartment and
met your old lover and
his friend on the way
out laughing.

I brought you a book
of poems that I love;
you have cooked
a simplified *coq au vin*.

The evening I decided to love you
you told me you loved me.

Passion declared.
Steak burned.

There is no future for us.
You have discovered the secret
that will bind me to you for life.

I returned.
You laughed.
When I answer my telephone
you are crying.

When I lived with you,
you spent your evenings
memorizing irregular
German verbs; now
that I spend my nights
investigating bamboo taxonomy,
you write that
I have ruined your life.

Daytona Beach Concert

The crippled violinist is bored, and
if he turns his eyes away from the young girls
in ball gowns, the husbands asleep,
the five hundred identical women in furs,
who will ask for a refund? We've been there ourselves,
one or two of us, around the chains
of identical tenements on Avenue D,
where the lame or the crazy or stupid are lost
and peculiar children sit in their empty rooms
to practice the violin, about all they're good for.
But if one has a gift, one may be saved
by the relatives coming to hear you play
Tartini's "Devil's Trill" like crazy at ten,
and your mother is proud of you, and your father
thanks God that even if you are a cripple
you might still amount to something, make money.
So you devote yourself to your art
ten, twelve hours a day, give your first recital
over the river at Carnegie, begin to make money,
and still play so well at times to yourself that
you remember the days in the spare room
when through the window spring invisible fumes
of exhausts and salt-sweetness from Brighton's ocean,
and you hear, far below you, laughter and curses
as the neighbor kids play punchball among trucks,
the voices shrill and excited, in spring,
by the vast possibilities of their impossible life;
so what can you do but play
Saint-Saëns' "Havanaise" like a madman chained to
    a rock?

But tonight, if he turns in contempt from his audience
to huddle over his third of Beethoven's "Archduke,"
who in this charity spectacle knows
he's not playing his best? Here even at midnight
automobiles prowl the vast stretches of beach,
and the pendulous breasts of the waves arrive
        unnoticed
to rub traces of footstep and tire
before the sun rises in his chains
to throw his gold into the ocean.

Anna Bachtle

Of course she's happy
in the kitchen
whose stone and metal
have been worn out by her flesh.
She's smoothed the clean linen
for fifty years;
in fall she laughs like a slice of moon
as she peels warm apples
into the battered colander in the sink.
The heavy cloth, the scent of fruit,
are comfortable things.
She is no appendix to her daughter's world.

Unless you escape in time,
she reviews forever the ancient pennants
on boats vanished from the river,
her first man's name,
the umbrella trees she saw one time in Kingston.
Seemingly content with chores,
with trees beyond the window
spinning familiar cycles,
she unfurls the wash like banners.
Surely her work is useful.
She earns her keep.
She tells her daughter's world as it runs
straight tracks toward its future,
"I am useful,
I am still here."

Zeno's Arrow

couldn't move, occupied
an infinity of points—
stationary at each—
or never passed them.
Either way,
motion is illusion.
The way to disprove his point
is to wing an arrow
to his heart.

The parrot fish, more subtle,
lives in a tawdry world
of coral and sharks.
Coral slowly builds its atolls;
sharks are "the perfect predatory machines."
Therefore the parrot fish
develops his nutcracker beak
with which he browses the coral
and, when ingested
by the prehistoric corporations of sharks,
gnaws his way through their bellies
to freedom.

Let us not discourse on change
but on the beautiful motions:
the arrows in their numerous trajectories,
the parrot fish in their jukebox cascades
of gold and blue and arsenic green,
not one identical to the other,
all of them seemingly satisfied,
not one of them argumentative.

III

I Wanted to Be a Ballerina

No matter that I was a plump child, chickenbreasted, with pigeon toes and goose flesh, it was the whirling hippo in *Fantasia* that fired me for Terpsichore. "But you're a boy," they said, "and you have a swinish case of psychosomatic gout to boot; give over these hapless dreams." Friends, I speak to you tonight as one who has conquered the quirks of circumstance and the incidents of birth. Laughter, pecker, phlebitis of my left leg have been overcome by the self-denial of toil; the thrifty sweat of industry has manured my barren ground. Therefore I accept your LL.D. with humility, but with pride. Thank you, Yale. America, close your eyes and you will see me dancing.

Faulty Ductwork

I have had faulty ductwork for years.
When I vacation, neighbors wire
DUCTWORK FAILING
WATER EVERYWHERE.
There have been three attempts at arson.
Invisible rowdies
throw stones at my mother.
The bats have vacated my house.
I have a burning sensation
when I urinate, and I am no longer
allowed to vote.
My oldest boy shoots up nurses,
and deer have deserted the meadow.
The specialists give estimates endlessly,
but there is never enough money
for repair.

Evolution

Last month I told myself I was a mountain
and smiled at the tourists who loved me.
I was a granite mountain, so sure of being
that the pines walked around me
and the daily winds broke up.
Two weeks ago I discovered
I was a wind-carved boulder
in equipoise
above myriad runways downhill.
You will not believe I'm about
to slide my knife in your ear
until I tell you that last week
I was a mud-colored bull hippopotamus
deciding whether to waddle to marshland
or charge the fire clouds rolling
while the sun melted down.

Machismo

Apes, a bunch of them,
above them swinging
an old one
squeezing apeshots
at their heads
while each youngster
fights for fruit rinds,
looks upward respectfully,
snarls,
vomits and eats it,
scratches his neighbor's back,
or curiously inspects
his asshole.

Marilyn says
you can tell the junior faculty there,
Dan says
and the director of the corporation,
but I'm interested
in the solitary baboon in the corner,
who sits on his hands and waits,
growing stronger every day,
gazing vacantly
at the apes.

At Kingston

We have come five hundred miles
to visit a pile of red bricks
dissolving in the golden afternoons.
The trash sumac almost hides the hollow windows
where great-grandfather
baked bread for the rich
above the flashing river.
Now even Blacks can't live in these ruins.
An investment trust, like history, knocks them flat,
and the powdery bricks are cast
over the palisade toward the river.
A mystery of old tires and bricks is lumped
beneath the sun-baked brow of the palisade.
Yesterday's river town, Kingston lies
like a menopausal old maid
betrayed by her bric-a-brac memories.

Here, where the death-loving sumac
spreads its dusty berries
through the black holes of the windows
and the fast-growing gold-green catalpas
are eaten by faster catalpa worms,
we have driven to reclaim great-grandpa,
a sour German with beeswaxed mustache,
in love with money and work.
For seventy years
that truculent immigrant stepped out of steerage
to squint appraisingly upward at Kingston,
the New World
where even garbage and the dead
are turned to gold.

Morte d'Arthur

When my cousin Arthur was alive,
he drove two Mercedes and a Lancia,
had an extra woman in Short Hills,
smoked opium hash in a gold pipe,
wore a Cuban cigar to my father's funeral,
was a friend of Duffy the Lark,
and ate mountains of fresh strawberries and yellow
    cream
in February at the head table in L'Overture's,
washing the mess down with Moët.

Now that my cousin Arthur is dead,
he lives with his mother's glaucoma,
packs machine-stamped hamburgers
in the Jiffy Meal factory in Hoboken,
masturbates in bus terminals,
squeezes pimples,
and sits staring at his hands.

He knows he is dead when he cuts his hands
and he bleeds.

The Inheritance

So, back to the lost paradise
after the neglect of fourteen years.
On the porch, at fourteen, I told my father
our condition resides within ourselves.
I had a red and white motorboat
to sail across the green-glazed patio
in autumn toward the wall of maples,
each golden on the edge of death.
Cousin Gunther sat on the patio,
telling us secrets and drinking
at noon; he knew the names of stars
and the proper names of toads,
and he is still alive somewhere,
a drunk repeating words to the green walls.
He was best at building giant snowmen
with basketball fists, and we
children, with round smoking mouths,
stood watching the old deciduous world,
innocently in love with snowmen,
and never thought
that fourteen years away,
we would still be standing,
arguing with prices in our mouths.
Little has changed,
except for the dead.
The trees offer up their golden leaves,
and a fat garden snake
squeezes into the dissolving wall.

Among His Effects We Found a Photograph

My mother is beautiful as a flapper.
She is so in love
that she has been gazing
secretly at my father
for forty years.
He's in uniform,
with puttees and swagger stick,
a tiny cork mustache
bobbing above a shore line of teeth.
They are "poor but happy."
In his hand is a lost book
he had memorized,
with a thousand clear answers
to everything.

Father at the Crematorium

His casket is fumed oak.
Cheeks rouged, mustache and nails
still growing, his thin lips
rest in set mockery;
as always, silence
is his last word.
My mother floats
like the ash of a burnt note
along the banks of flowers.
Distant relatives
whisper politely about money.
Two attendants laugh
to kill time in the anteroom.

At last I understand his stillness.
Now his nails curl into my palms,
his snarl grows in my throat.
Buried all his life in his body
was a lost mine that explodes in the fire.

Taking a Greyhound on an Impulse
to Oklahoma City

For Bill Korbel

My heart is a comic *bandido*
with a gold tooth and pecker tracks
and half-moon smile:
"Come on, come on, I won't hurt you!"
says the terror of the Sierra Madre.

Waking in the Greyhound Station in Oklahoma City
with a three-day growth,
hamburger grease on my teeth,
and penis shriveled
like a peyote button lost in the mud,
it is like waking up on the edge
of a grave you have dug
waiting for the soldiers to shoot
but expecting that the governor
will send a reprieve and also
a large annuity for life:
"Wait, wait, *señores,*
there has been some mistake!"

My Teeth

The up-front ones are marvelous,
tiny dancers braving the wind,
shapely and disciplined.
But behind them, corruption,
molars who have lived riotously,
roots eaten by secret lusts
as their bodies disintegrate .
Even the bicuspids and incisors
are infected,
blood swollen
around stiff afflictions of plaque.

The stains of drugs and nicotine
have reached behind the skirts of the dancers,
and it is only a matter of time
before the curtain comes down for good
and the closed mouth
fosters a strange revolution,
the muffled tongue rising
like a brutalized peasantry
to taste its own power
at last.

My Penis

Ordinarily I call it "my cock," but
often there is a strange formality about it,
this rocket with wattles.
"Penis" and "Vagina," a dignified couple
immobile on a Grecian urn
or at times engaged in elegant ballet and
desiring frequent medical checkups.
"Cock" and "Twat," two funloving kids
traveling from Pittsburgh to Tangiers
with a hundred bucks in their pockets,
laughing at Baptists but loving God.

Alone, it's
crazy and laughable, like the man
who stands up at every Quaker meeting,
testifying to his version of the Truth—
a drag to others but a private solace,
refusing to sit down when others whisper
"shush," "shame," "time and place for everything"—
a dotty old turkey continually rising in wonder,
even on lonely winter evenings refusing
not to point to the stars.

Note for Door

Today when I woke
you were gone
and I
was like a salesman
in a small-town hotel room
drunk on loneliness
and listening to laughter
next door
and I was
a boy scout marooned
in a dry-rotted cabin
by the greatest snowstorm
even seen in northern Vermont
listening to strange birds
scratching the roof
and I was
a man coming home
to his house full of children
and finding nothing there
but the echoes of his scream.

I am going out now
to look at
the green ducks
paddle nowhere
on the river
but if you should return
while I'm out marking time
this is to tell you
I'm home.

The Gift

One day
as I was lying on the lawn
dreaming of the Beautiful
and my wife was justifiably bitching
    out the window
at my shiftlessness and
the baby was screaming
because I wouldn't let him
eat my cigarettes,
a tiger cat leaped over the fence,
smiled at my wife,
let the baby pull his tail,
hummed like a furry dynamo
as I stroked him.

My wife took the car to get him some food,
my son began to sing his wordless song,
and I wrote a poem in the sand.

Now God give every man who's hopeless
a beautiful wife,
an infant son who sings,
and the gift of a sweet-faced cat.

A Line of Patchen's

You were asleep
behind the golden mask
of your hair.

The winter rain
drains away
through our lawn
of sand.

The child
is struggling
against his enemy,
sleep.

I love you so much
that war will die.

Ordinary Evening

In our obscure life, for instance, how easy
it is to turn from the masters falling into the sea.
No doubt they were amazing—
the whiteness of their legs in the green water!—
but it is not an important failure.
The living eat a cold peach
delicious from the refrigerator or
cleanse the intricate joints of an engine
in pure gasoline, and its vapors rise
like barely visible snakes
finally lost in the sun.
It is also good
to teach a child to sing
with words or without,
to love and afterwards
go slowly hand in hand
for a swim in the astringent ocean.

How to Get Here

The sun rises above the Expressway East;
follow that until noon.
At the fork in the road by the overturned semi,
go left, north by northwest.
A young woman with a lantern
will be seen walking along Route 156.
Follow her past a barn
with a broken reaper.
At a springhouse, go right
as the moon rises and past
an abandoned mineshaft.
Where the arrow for old Route 210
points left, go straight up the hill
past the man with the shotgun
obliterating roadsigns.
At the top of the hill
there is an abandoned schoolhouse.
Inside is an elderly man in the dark,
cataloguing antiques.
Be sure to approach him with a gift.
He has never met us but knows
we are here.

Facts about Death

Richard Farina dove off a bridge at night in Ithaca and six years later broke his neck by driving his bike into a tree in California.

When my father died I remembered that one day in a Chinese restaurant above the Ridgewood Theater he sneezed chow mein.

I have been crying for six years about Farina.

I am about to buy a schoolhouse built in 1879. On the foundation is scratched "DK." Bob Step, who will sell it for $600, went to school there. Now he can't get into it because of the bees.

I don't believe anything that Farina said. The Cuban story, the peyote milkshake from the dark man. I think Kristin was either the daughter of the Swedish ambassador or the girl from Alexandria with the mole on her upper lip.

When he saw asparagus growing he said, "They look like green pricks coming out of the earth." Farina said, "The dead are trying to tell us something."

Outside the schoolhouse the pokeweed is growing. In the fall their berries are dark as drops of old blood. Poisonous. The old plant contains phytolaccin, causing paralysis, but also long used as a medicinal herb.

When they arise in the spring they look and taste like asparagus.

The Elizabethans ripened apricots in dung and believed asparagus was an aphrodisiac, undoubtedly because of the phallic suggestions.

The night Farina returned I got to make it with the girl from Alexandria but, being drunk, couldn't get one up. "Poor thing, poor thing, it's all right, I understand," yawning.

My grandmother said, "You have to understand your father." I've given it all up. When my mother found him on the lawn he was serious as always. Cause of death: digging weeds.

When I die I would like to be in that schoolhouse among the poke plants, children and friends around me, bees overhead, everybody laughing. I would like to read them this and go underground laughing.